Meet the NEW ENGLAND PATRIOTS

PERCY LEED

Lerner Publications ◆ Minneapolis

Copyright © 2026 by Lerner Publishing Group, Inc.

Stats in this book are accurate through the 2024 National Football League season.

All rights reserved. International copyright secured. No part of this book may be reproduced, stored in a retrieval system, or transmitted in any form or by any means—electronic, mechanical, photocopying, recording, or otherwise—without the prior written permission of Lerner Publishing Group, Inc., except for the inclusion of brief quotations in an acknowledged review.

Lerner Publications Company
An imprint of Lerner Publishing Group, Inc.
241 First Avenue North
Minneapolis, MN 55401 USA

For reading levels and more information, look up this title at www.lernerbooks.com.

Main body text set in ITC Avant Garde Gothic Std.
Typeface provided by Adobe Systems.

Editor: Annie Zheng **Designer:** Mary Ross
Lerner team: Sue Marquis

Library of Congress Cataloging-in-Publication Data

Names: Leed, Percy, 1968- author.
Title: Meet the New England Patriots / Percy Leed.
Description: Minneapolis : Lerner Publications, 2026. | Series: Lerner sports rookie. Terrific teams | Includes bibliographical references and index. | Audience: Ages 5–8 | Audience: Grades K-1 | Summary: "The New England Patriots are home to some of the NFL's best players, including Tom Brady, Matthew Judon, and James White. Learn about the team's best moments, stats, and more"— Provided by publisher.
Identifiers: LCCN 2024043935 (print) | LCCN 2024043936 (ebook) | ISBN 9798765668450 (library binding) | ISBN 9798765683682 (paperback) | ISBN 9798765681855 (epub)
Subjects: LCSH: New England Patriots (Football team)—History—Juvenile literature.
Classification: LCC GV956.N36 L44 2026 (print) | LCC GV956.N36 (ebook) | DDC 796.332/640974461—dc23/eng/20240926

LC record available at https://lccn.loc.gov/2024043935
LC ebook record available at https://lccn.loc.gov/2024043936

Manufactured in the United States of America
1-1011740-53813-3/20/2025

Photo Acknowledgments
Jaiden Tripi/Getty Images, p. 5; AP Photo, p. 7; Stan Honda/AFP via Getty Images, p. 9; Al Bello/Getty Images, p. 11; Al Pereira/Getty Images/Michael Ochs Archives/Getty Images, p. 13; Jeff Haynes/AFP via Getty Images, p. 14; Jim Davis/The Boston Globe via Getty Images, p. 16; Focus on Sport/Getty Images, p. 19; Damian Strohmeyer via AP, p. 20; Winslow Townson/Getty Images, p. 22; Hunter Martin/Getty Images, p. 23. Design elements: Kwangmoozaa/Getty Images; Andrii Shelenkov/Getty Images; AnthiaCumming/Getty Images. Cover: AP Photo/Michael Dwyer.

Table of Contents

Chapter 1 The Patriots 4

Chapter 2 Big Moments 8

Chapter 3 Best Players 12

Chapter 4 Do Your Job 18

New England Patriots Team Leaders 23

Glossary 24

Learn More 24

Index 24

CHAPTER 1
The Patriots

The New England Patriots were losing to the New York Jets. With 22 seconds left in the game, Rhamondre Stevenson scored for the Patriots. The Patriots won 25–22!

Rhamondre Stevenson

The Patriots became a team in 1959.

They played in Boston, Massachusetts.
Their name was the Boston Patriots.

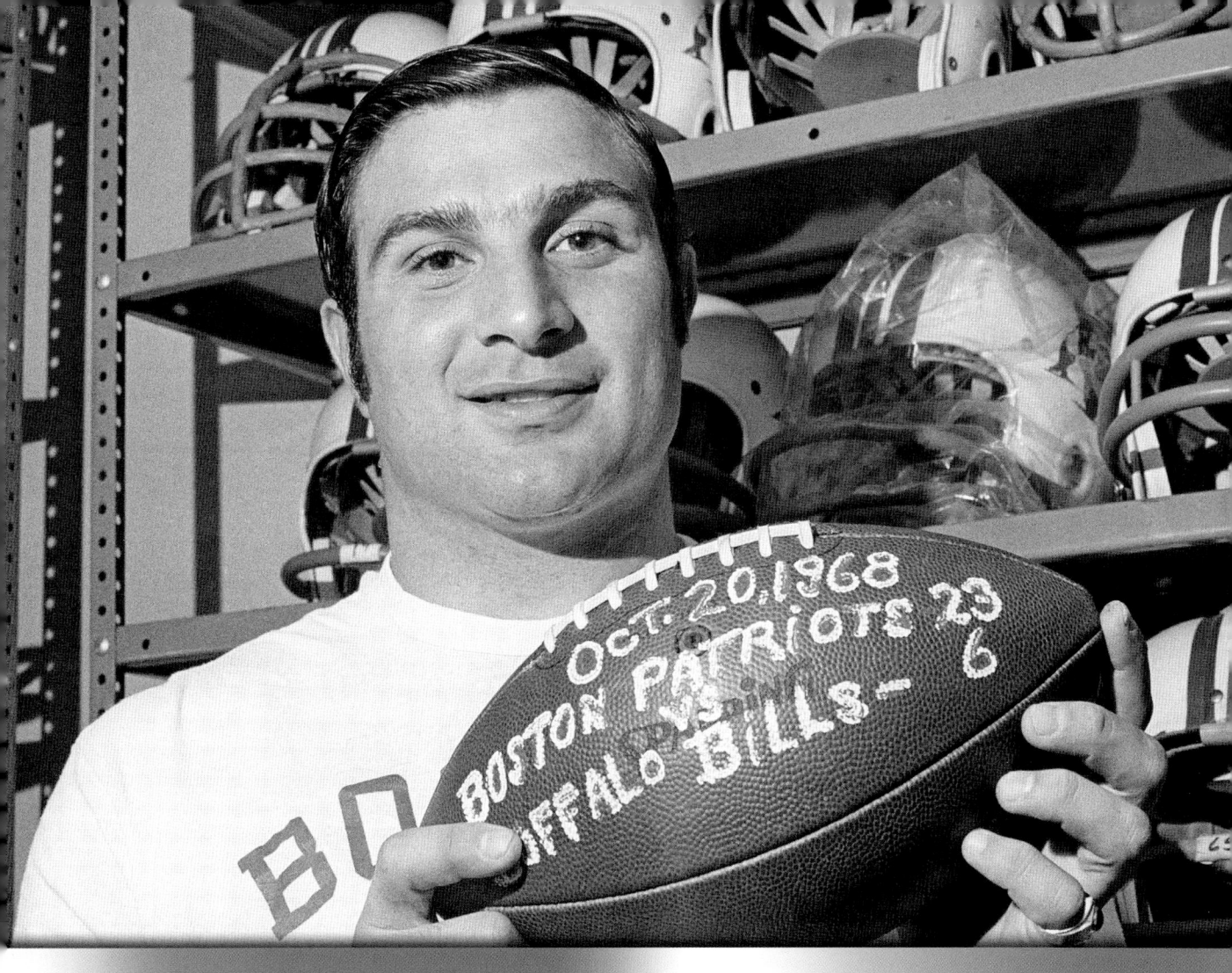

In 1971, the Patriots moved to Foxborough, Massachusetts. They changed their name to the New England Patriots.

CHAPTER 2
Big Moments

The Patriots didn't do well at first. Then, in 1976, they had their best season with 11 wins.

In 2002, the Patriots won their first Super Bowl. They beat the St. Louis Rams 20–17.

In 2007, the Patriots became the fourth team in NFL history to win all their games in the regular season.

The 2019 Super Bowl was a tough game. The Patriots and Los Angeles Rams were tied. Then the Patriots scored and won 13–3.

CHAPTER 3
Best Players

John "Hog" Hannah was a star on offense. His blocking helped the Patriots set a new NFL record for rushing yards in 1978.

Quarterback Drew Bledsoe played for the Patriots from 1993 to 2001. He is the second-best passer in the team's history.

Tom Brady is the greatest quarterback in NFL history. He won six Super Bowls with the Patriots.

Dont'a Hightower is a tough defender. He helped the Patriots win three Super Bowls.

James White

Running back James White is an all-star. In 2017, he set an NFL record for most catches in a Super Bowl game.

Quarterback Drake Maye is a rising star. He threw 15 touchdown passes for New England in 2024.

CHAPTER 4
Do Your Job

The Patriots have won six Super Bowls. They are tied for the most wins with the Pittsburgh Steelers.

The Patriots' motto is "do your job." This means that each player walks onto the field ready to do their best.

The team has not had much success in the 2020s.

The Patriots hope to get better in the next few seasons. With this team, anything is possible.

NEW ENGLAND PATRIOTS TEAM LEADERS

Passing touchdowns: Tom Brady, 541
Passing yards: Tom Brady, 74,571
Receiving touchdowns: Rob Gronkowski, 79
Rushing yards: Sam Cunningham, 5,453
Rushing touchdowns: Jim Nance, 45

Glossary

motto: a phrase that the team follows

NFL: National Football League

Pro Bowl: the NFL's all-star game

Learn More

Downs, Kieran. *Football*. Minneapolis: Bellwether Media, 2024.

Flynn, Brendan. *Football*. Minneapolis: Early Encyclopedias, 2024.

Leed, Percy. *Football's Super Bowl*. Minneapolis: Lerner Publications, 2025.

Index

Boston Patriots, 6

quarterback, 13–14, 17

record, 12, 16

Super Bowl, 9, 11, 14–16, 18